To
Truely enjoyed
the Reunion & seeing
you & the others!
Hope To make it again
Pat

Rhymes of
a Family Doctor

Dr. Danny Sullivan

American Literary Press, Inc.
Baltimore, Maryland

Rhymes of a Family Doctor

Library of Congress
Cataloging in Publication Data
ISBN 1-56167-163-0

Published by

American Literary Press, Inc.
8019 Belair Road, Suite 10
Baltimore, Maryland 21236

Manufactured in the United States of America

To my wife, Helen
"You Decorated My Life"

Table of Contents

Introduction	*ix*
Aknowledgments	*xi*

Grandfathers are Old	1
The Sun and the Stick	2
In the Park	3
On the Beach	4
The Rabbit and the Carrot	5
Little Bundle of Joy	6
The Little Artist	7
The Man of Their Dreams	8
A Little Gift of Life	9
Two Butterflies and a Rose	10
The Little Red Bike	11
The Rock and a Ball	12
The Youth Center	14
Life of a Teenager	15
Adolescent Form	16
The Leprechaun's Gold	17
Epidemic of Green	18
The Irish Fiddler	19
Danny Boy	20
Buffalo Bill's Knee	22
Fifty Fearless Men	23
Memorial Day	24
The Star Spangled Banner	26
Mother's Day	27
Ghosts and Goblins	28
Thanksgiving	29

The Harvest and Thanksgiving	30
Election Day	31
Don't Eat the Cookies	32
Christmas Eve	34
Santa Won't Come Christmas Day	36
Hospital Christmas	37
Christmas Celebration	38
Mother Poem	39
Annie	40
My Poetry	41
The Dictionary	42
Down Through the Ages	43
Chameleon	44
I Almost... Maybe... Saw a Flying Saucer	45
Up in the Artic	48
The Armored Vests	49
Mother Nature	50
Sunshine	51
The Leaf	52
Golf	53
A Fish Story That's True	55
The Gulf	56
Doctor My Doctor	57
The Fingernail	58
Malpractice	59
Holding Life's Hand	60
His Life Was His Family	61
Alice May	62
The Need For A Smoke	63
The Newborn	66
Pitocin	67

The Gallbladder 68
Fever and Cough 69
The Wee and the Bee 70
Government and Insurance 71
Wait Before Light 72
Five to Nine 74
The Doctor is a Lady 75
The Stroke 76
The Guardian Angels 77
A Life of Service 78
A Lifetime of Effort 79
The Phobia 80
Divorce 81
The Forgotten Father 83
She's Pretty and She's Spunky 85
The Sixteenth of January 86
The Wedding Toast 87
Yourself You are Filled 88
My Needs are Not Great 89
Chains on the Mind 90
My Sister Rose 91
Triplets 92
The Flashing Red Light 93
The Year Twenty-Nine 94
The Man From Toledo 95
The Girl in My Dream 97
The Best That You Can Be 99
Skied Down the Hill 100
Money 101
A Father and a Friend 102
I Feel 103

The Pharmaceutical Rep   104
Sixty Years Old   105
Life Can Be True   107
Little Pete   108
The Grain Feeder   109
Carcinoma   110
Sports Doctor   111
1994   112
The Skater   113
The Racer   114

About the Author   115

Introduction

I've been addicted to reading everything within my grasp as long as I can remember. Poetry, humor, and good stories have always had a very special attraction for me. Poetry with strong metaphors are special. The selection of a powerful word at the start or the end of a line grasps and holds my attention. I consider reading poetry aloud as a good test of its flavor.

As a Family Physician for over thirty years, a great deal of my time has been spent in explaining medical problems or giving directions in language that the patient can readily understand.

Many tales of the past and best remembered stories have had the flavor of a rhyme. With all this in mind, I selected the rhyme as a tool for many of my stories. Many of my creations are stories, tales, or recordings of moments in time. They are an attempt to share a feeling, event, or thought that many have experienced in themselves. It is hoped that some readers will be able to identify with the images that are created in these writings. When the verse describes a medical condition, it is either one that has happened many times or is changed to fit no one special.

My patients, friends and family have encouraged this book. I hope that you have as much fun reading it as I did in writing it.

Acknowledgments

I would like to thank all of the wonderful people who have read my rhymes and encouraged me through this effort. Especially, I would like to thank our office manager, Myrna who has read them all, Alice May, Cheryl and Molly who work and put up with me every day, and the rest of the Fallen Timbers staff. All of the comments from patients, pharmaceutical reps and others have been appreciated. The members of "The Writers' Company" where I have read many of my rhymes have been supportive.

Especially I wish to thank my wife, Helen, my friends including Sue, Bud, Bill and Lynn for tolerating the good and the not so good rhymes in process. It mostly started with a rhyme to "Mr. Bud" which is not included in this book. If this work is accepted and liked, he will be in a future book in an expanded version which is already being written.

Grandfathers are Old

Grandfathers are old, sometimes very smart
They are usually overweight but have a big heart
Grandfathers are tired, and they've lived a long time
But catch them just right, and they'll tell you a rhyme

Grandfather was sleeping, laid out in his chair
The sound of his snoring resounded through the air
Three little children crept quietly across the room
They didn't want to disturb him, not yet, but pretty soon

They crept up into his lap and snuggled down close
Soon that became boring, and more active thoughts arose
They started to giggle and poke at his side
Soon the snoring stopped, and his eyes opened wide

They wanted a story that only grandfathers can tell
They pleaded and begged, even started to yell
They settled down quickly, when he started to speak
Their little hands were gently touching his elderly cheek

The Sun and the Stick

Once upon a time a long time ago
There was this deep dense forest where children seldom go.
Three little children ran and played that day
They talked and they laughed and soon lost their way.

They looked all around and searched in every direction.
But all they could see was forest and no path for selection
They argued and cried, pointed this way and that.
But no one really knew where they were so they sat.

They sat on a log and tried to remember.
How they came through the forest with Grandfather last
September
They had been told that if careful you could usually find your way
You simply need to remain calm and travel by day

What would Grandfather do if he lost his way??
He wasn't here when they needed him on this playtime day
The little girl suddenly remembered a story about a stick and
the sun
Soon the boys remembered too, and they were soon having fun

Place a stick on the ground and point it at the sun
Hide the shadow so the stick and the shadow are one
Draw a circle around it and wait for the shadow to run from the stick
It points to the east then just take your pick

The forest is south of their home they did know
So using east for a reference to the north they did go
Soon they came out of the forest and arrived at their home
Grandfather, Grandfather we've a story to do
It's about the sun, a stick, the forest and you

In the Park

They walked to the park
They ran down the path
They were there with Grandfather
They played and they laughed

He was getting kind of old
He was becoming very slow
But a day spent with Grandfather
Was fun and they wanted to go

He listened when they talked
He smiled as they did play
He marveled at their energy
As they played in the park that day

He never seemed to rush them
He was gentle, caring and kind
He made them feel important
Knew what was on their mind

On the Beach

They sat on the beach
They played in the sand
They build little castles
They worked on their tan

At the end of the day
The water came in
They'd come back tomorrow
And build their castles again

The water comes in
And the water goes out
They went to their Grandfather
To find what it's all about

The playing was over
They sat by his side
The sun was now setting
Water rose with the tide

The Rabbit and the Carrot

The rabbit dug and grasped the carrot
Then he ran and leaped into his hole
Storing enough carrots for the Winter
And then some was his ultimate goal

His family had lived in the garden
For several generations and more
Stealing the old gardener's carrots
To eat and some for Winter to store

The gardener had always then chased him
Sometimes it was really quite close
One time he almost had grabbed him
But just missed and bloodied his nose

This grab and chase daily contest
Accumulating carrots and sometimes a tear
The rabbit always obtained enough carrots
Which lasted throughout the long year

Grandfather had always planted more carrots
Then he ever really could want
Because even though he chased these little bunnies
He simply enjoyed seeing them jump

Little Bundle of Joy

They chased him, they grabbed him
They threw him in his bed
He couldn't understand
Why they wouldn't play instead

It was three o'clock in the morning
He was rested and feeling quite well
Why his parents needed to sleep
He couldn't ever really tell

During the day they were busy
Just being practicing adults
At night there's more opportunity
For attention and the fun that results

There's no one else to consider
Just this active energetic little boy
But why do they no longer call him
Their little "Bundle of Joy"

The Little Artist

The room was quiet. The room was small
The new little artist had created it all
Using the media at hand, he drew on the wall
Images and pictures that he hoped
Would please all

The media he had, he applied with his hand
Reached for some more, supply and demand
He was just about finished, when to his surprise
The door to the room opened
It was followed by a cry

His drawing was terminated as quick as can be
She didn't appreciate it, as he could readily see
She picked up the dirty diaper that lay by the wall
Cleaned up the little artist and his creation on the wall

The Man of Their Dreams

They really like chubby
But drink "diet light"
They sat around the table
Then screamed with delight

Across the floor
Came the man of their dreams
He danced and he pranced
In his very tight jeans

His belly stuck way out
In the front
And when he turned around
He had is little tiny rump

Just when they thought
They had finally seen it all
He dropped all his clothes
And stood very tall

Then to provide them
With one more tiny joy
The little two year old bent over
And picked up his toy

A Little Gift of Life

A little gift of life just came running
Through my front door
This little gift has two hands
Two legs and ever so much more

The little gift leaped up into my arms
Grabbed me around the neck
And held on ever so tight
I don't know whose heart was fluttering
more
But it all seemed fantastically right

Life has many blessings
And if just one could come true
Is having a little grandchild
Who especially loves you

Two Butterflies and a Rose

New Life Symbol
One is just for that
Old life, new direction
The second for the life to last

Thorns along the way
Difficult but protective too
A beautiful life in the future
The flower shows it's true

The Little Red Bike

This was the day, the day of the test
No longer a toddler, the toys put to rest
Two wheels on a bike, not stable three
Time to stand up, an older child you see
The bike's colored red, the seat it is black
Riding a new two wheeler, it's a "primal" attack
The families are on the sidewalk and gathered around
It's the day to stand up and ride on new ground
We hold the bike for him and he sits on the seat
We'll give him a good start, no need to repeat
Away he does go,.... gee he peddles fast
Riding that two wheeler is a difficult task

Halfway down the block the child takes a fall
We all rush to help him, parents one and all
Off to the ER, this group did then go
He was examined and treated, everything just so
A big bright clean cast suddenly appears
He is crying but smiling as we all gather near

No longer a toddler, he's now a big child
He's ridden his bike and his injuries are mild
He walks with a strut, his confidence has grown
He'll ride his new bike with hardly a moan
Showing off his cast, his arm will soon heal
He'll enjoy his red bike on only two wheels

The Rock and a Ball

The small child walked slowly down the block
He bounced a ball and played with a rock
He wished that he was big like the older boy next door
He'd then bounce the ball and run up the score

He practiced the moves, the jumps and really tried hard
The little boy with the rock and the ball out in his yard
He bounced the ball, played with his rock and more
The little guy trying to be just like the big boy next door

The big boy next door bounced and passed the ball around
He played with his friends running over the ground
They took a peach basket and used it for a hoop
Learned to play the game by the chickens in their coop

Down the street bigger boys played at the school
Bigger and better plays, practice was the rule
Five on each side, really big league now
To make the bigger team, they'd do it somehow

Inside the High School, uniforms and all
No more peach basket, and a regulation ball
They practice their shots and some make the team
Competing in sports is every boys' dream

Games to be won, games to be lost
Finish the season at a physical cost
Those who are great play college next year
Talk about competitive, the demands are severe

NCAA and the season is over
If you win that one your life is in clover
The scouts will come around and stand by your door
Offer you the moon and even much more

On to the Pros, full time, full court
Only the best can finish the sort
Then famous and wealthy if dreams do come true
But you start with a peach basket, a ball and rock too

The Youth Center

Lonely girl, Lonely girl, you're doing your time
You are out of circulation, so I'll write you a rhyme
A teenager's lament, "I promise to be good"
You are now housed by the county in a home made of wood
She is missing her family, her friends and her lad
She doesn't want to be lonely, bedraggled or sad

She tested the rules and the law it is said
She ran away to be free. Now it's prison instead
Teenager, Teenager, she longs to be free
She'll abide by the rules. A model student you'll see
Following the rules, she is learning how to cope
She'll become an adult and be responsible we hope

Lonely girl, Lonely girl, doing your time
Out of circulation, I'll write you a rhyme
Down deep in her heart she wants to be good
She's housed by the county in that house made of wood
We love her and we care for her. She is a pretty young lass
When she rejoins the world, she'll do it with class

Life of a Teenager

The life of a teenager is difficult at best
Everyday something happens putting it to the test
Growing up is hard, it can even be a drag
Facing daily challenges, go forward, please don't lag

Down beneath the surface the character is there
Strong as an ox, no time to despair
Push away that depression, keep the energy high
Feel good about yourself, don't even breathe a sigh

Your image is good, independent and strong
Depending on others can sometimes be wrong
Learn to like yourself, the feeling is good
Develop independence as a normal teenager should

Adolescent Form

Standing before the mirror time after time
Studying each little crevice, every little line
Growing and glowing, this new body appears
Looking it over, studying what has to last for years
No longer a child, this interesting emerging life form
Studying it for hours is an adolescent norm

There are many new feelings deep down inside
Urges to consider, rules to test or abide
Wake up and shout, the new teenager exclaims
New worlds to explore, new behavior to tame
Sometimes aggressive, sometimes very shy
Not simply delicious, like Mom's apple pie
Whatever the behavior, it's all accepted now
The main things the image, that doesn't bend or bow

The image is good, the appearance is sad
Never satisfied with appearance, needs improving a tad
Time to talk with friends, no tale is to wild
Explore different behaviors, please keep it mild
Setting new goals, tasks must be done
Learning all things a teenager needs on the run
Sometimes an adult, sometimes a child
To adults they seem crazy, unpredictable and wild

It's hard being an adolescent, the ups and the downs
Learning all that's needed to function out on the town
Now comes the day adolescent is remote
Sooner or later, they all become adults

The Leprechaun's Gold

Once Upon a time a long time ago
On that little green isle where all want to go
Lived wee little people Leprechauns by name
Hoarding the gold was their main claim to fame

Searchers did come, and searchers did go
Never did they find that big pot of gold
Leprechauns are wise and treasured their gold
Then decided to share it with the Irish I'm told
To some they gave songs, poetry and prose
To all they gave the blarney, creative and bold

The rest of the gold they stored in the stone
It's up in the castle and sits all alone
A bit of the blarney, delightful and bold
A rare gift from the ancients, the ancients of old
Now all who might kiss that rare blarney stone
May come away richer with some Leprechaun's gold

Epidemic of Green

An epidemic occurs each year in the spring
A gathering of the Irish, the most ever seen
They all wear the shamrock, a very good sign
Celebrating the spring, and have a good time

It's the time of the Irish, all over the globe
This three leaf green clover, symbolic I'm told
For those who have wondered what these three leaves
might mean
It all started one year with the green of the spring

The first leaf for spring, new life has begun
Three cheers to the green, we do it as one
The second leaf for surviving the winter just past
It's now just behind us, we think we can last

The third leaf's for hope, we'll start a new year
Complete it again, and drink some green beer
So here's to the Irish who celebrate spring
Sign of the shamrock, and the wearing of the green

The Irish Fiddler

My Grandfather played the Irish Fiddle
He played as good as can be
He always played at the Iowa Fair
Just good enough to be second you see

He practiced and how he could fiddle
He competed and played every year
But whenever the contest was over
Always Second Fiddle to his peer

Happy, this Irishman played on his fiddle
He continued to be second you see
His friends laughed and they teased him
First Fiddle was always little brother "Timothy"

Danny Boy

The whistle of the train sounded over my head
An image of my childhood surfaced in my mind
A group of small children
Ran across the field
Our custom was to go to the sale barn
There were many animals, people and
Adventures for us children
This day we wandered
Past the barn complex
Walked down to the tracks by the creek
Laughing and teasing
We climbed the trestle of the bridge
Sitting on one of the concrete pillars
We felt very powerful and even wicked
Being at this forbidden site
A copy of a Sears catalog was found
Left by some mysterious visitor
One of the boys had a cigarette
We all took our turn

We climbed down the trestle
Ran to swim in the creek
I was only six
My brother was eight
I waded out
The other boys could swim

I stood on my toes
Going Deeper
The bottom was soft and mucky
Suddenly, it was very deep

Images ran through my mind
Tarzan swimming up through the depths
Jane in his arms
A hand on my wrist
Broke the flow of my dream
I was jerked to the surface
Gasping
My dream had been broken

Exhausted, I waded to the shore
Quiet, embarrassed
We returned home
Nothing was ever said
Boys do forbidden things
They don't tell parents
Or others

The boy who saved me
I never forgot
We had sung in school
The day before the swim
He sang a solo
Sitting right beside me
Turning my face red
He sang "Danny Boy"

Buffalo Bill's Knee

My mother sat on Bill Cody's knee
He'd tell her great stones
About her grandfather and he
They'd served in the Civil War
They scouted then out west
And the stories that he told
Were simply the very best

His circus was now famous
He had traveled near and far
But he always stopped at their house
Once he came in a motor car

Grandmother she had known him
Since she was just a little child
She'd grown up along the Platte
Even stayed at his ranch a while
He was now a famous showman
Known around the world was he
But when he came to Des Moines
My mother sat upon his knee

Fifty Fearless Men

The tale of the *Fearless Fifty*
Researched and recorded in time
The exploits of the *Fearless Fifty*
Impossible to present as a rhyme

There was is man named Orvel Criqui
Historian and recorder of fact
He researched all sides of the battle
The scouts and the warriors who attacked

His book will long be a reference
On Beecher's Island and tales of the west
But it's the part about my ancestor
That I like but still read the rest

The Indians were lead by Roman Nose
The scouts commanded by Major Forsyth
After the three day battle was over
Some were dead and some were alive

The results of the battle are debated
Each side claims to really have won
But no one can protest the courage
Of both sides, each and every one

(The Battle of Beecher's Island
Sept. 17-20, 1868)

Based on the book <u>Fifty Fearless Men</u>
by Orvel Criqui (Walsworth Pub., Marceline, MO)

23

Memorial Day

"Four score and seven years ago"
These words are often spoken
It's a time to remember
The survivors, the dead and the broken

Memorial Day is a special moment in time
Honoring those who have served
For their country, each in their time

Some veterans bore arms
Some veterans did not
But each served their country
And accepted their lot

We remember the battles
We remember the foes
We forget the politicians
Who created these woes

The Revolution, Brandywine
The Paoli Massacre
Wyoming Valley, Fallen Timbers
That one was fought here

1812, The Black Hawk War
And then The North and South
That Civil War that brought the tears
An he said "Four Score and Seven Years"

A special day to remember
To honor the brave and the dead
We call is day Memorial Day
Remembering all who have bled

Now there's many more wars to remember
The list gets longer with time
I'd much rather remember the old ones
No new ones would suit me just fine

The Star Spangled Banner

I went to this city down by the sea
Business in the city and history to see
Out on the bay was located this fort
Ft. McHenry of old, and history to report
The War of 1812 was a special event
So out to that fort I eagerly went

There were battles and skirmishes a long time ago
And a man wrote a song that we all do love so
On the land and the sea, even out on the plain
The British they fought creating much pain
But the song that was written down by the sea
The Star Spangled Banner by Francis Scott Key

Mother's Day

Twas the tenth of May
Her sons were all grown
Twas Sunday and Mother's Day
She would celebrate alone

They hadn't forgot her
But the world it did call
Getting on with their lives
It happens to us all

She raised them, they loved her
They've become two fine sons
And they love her no less
But don't live with her as one

It's a mother's vocation
To raise and let go
She will celebrate this Mother's Day
For being able to do so

Ghosts and Goblins

Ghosts and goblins are all around the town
Stalking the city is the Baskerville Hound
Many little people are strolling all costumed
Look out little children, the monsters are exhumed

Up to the door and quickly ring the bell
It's trick or it's treat, exciting stories to tell
The devil is lurking, and no one knows where
Happy goblins abound, they're doing their share

Just get through the night and bag all the treats
But when it gets late, please clear the streets
Early evening is fun but later it will change
Better be home early, safe... and suffer no pain

Halloween is a time for treats and certainly fun
Later, it will be tricks so you had better run
The goblins and ghosts will soon go away
But they will be back come next Halloween day

Thanksgiving

Bless this family, this food and this
very special day
Let us each give thanksgiving in our own
or special way
Each and everyone be thankful
all who are here
Bless and be thankful for another special year

The Harvest and Thanksgiving

Bless this family, food and friends
At this harvest time of year
Bless this day we call Thanksgiving
With those that we hold dear

May the next year fulfill our wishes
May we gather once again
Thanksgiving is a time for sharing
With our family and our friends

Election Day

The time was November
First Tuesday was the day
We all got up early
We voters have our say

There were issues and that candidate
We'll pull levers by the score
Politics and issues, decisions to be made
Should we vote them down, or let them
have more

Complications? government? frustrating to us
Asking for our vote, more money and such
The system is full of riddles and really confusing polls
But the "right to vote" comes from our very souls

Our system has problems, we often do complain
Between each election, are problems and pain
But come election Tuesday, a big November day
We vote for change, that's the "American Way"

Don't Eat the Cookies

I parked in the drive, Burst through the door
The smell of baking struck me and I sat on the floor
My eyes lit up like Christmas tree lights
The aroma had me salivating with all of my might

I walked into the kitchen, a marvelous site to see
The room was filled with cookies
And probably just for me
The table was filled, the counters covered too
The oven still was baking, that meant more cookies due

I reached across the table to grab a sampled few
This voice it came from behind me
My hand still empty withdrew
"DON'T EAT THE COOKIES" the voice it did say
One listens to that voice, to cross it never does pay

My face turned red but I looked for a way
"DO YOU SUPPOSE I could have one?
Would that be OK?"
The voice still resounded as I meekly left the room
No cookies now but maybe pretty soon

The house became quiet, everyone in bed
I crept to the kitchen with "COOKIE THOUGHTS"
in my head
Every kind of cookie, all colors and special taste
To not simply try one would certainly be a waste

I listened for a while and didn't hear a sound
Lifted up the cover with no one else around
"DON'T EAT THE COOKIES" the paper did say
It was printed in bright red so I'll wait another day

I got up in the morning, all the cookies were gone
They were packed up in big boxes as gifts with
wrappings on
I was feeling dejected as I went about that day
All those freshly baked cookies, There simply
had to be a way

When I came home and slowly walked through the door
No more aroma, No cookies by the score
But sitting there upon the table, a package just for me
It was filled with lots of cookies, as I could plainly see

The card on the package, My name I could plainly see
It said "EAT THE COOKIES" and they were
just for me

Christmas Eve

The moon was shining through
The trees and falling snow
Large snow flakes gently settling
Making moon beam after glow

The wind gently blowing
Through the trees and their leaves
A wonderful night for sleeping
A beautiful Christmas Eve

The lights in the windows
Some shinning, some are twinkling
Lots of colors and music
A Christmas rhapsody I am thinking

Inside the house
All decorated and bright
Everyone in good spirits
On this very special night

All are a slumber
The children tried to stay awake
But on this Christmas night
All have to sleep for goodness sake

He comes in the night
No one really knows when
But each and every year
He leaves and returns again

He's out of the house
Before he seems to be in
It happens so fast
Like a blink in the wind

His sleigh it is long
Pulled by tiny reindeer
For it's all around the world
Bringing presents and cheer

If you put out a snack
It will always be gone
It takes lots of energy on
A night that's this long

And if you listen close
As he blinks out of sight
The star trail will tell you
It is a Merry Christmas Night

Santa Won't Come Christmas Day

Don't eat the candy
The voices they do say
If you eat the fresh wrapped candy
Santa won't come Christmas Day

Don't eat the cookies
The voices they do say
If you eat the fresh baked cookies
Santa won't come Christmas day

Don't leave your chores uncompleted
The voices they do say
If you don't complete your chores
Santa won't come Christmas Day

Be good and do your school work
The voices they do say
If you don't complete your school work
Santa won't come Christmas Day

Obey the rules. Obey your parents
The voices they do say
If you don't love and obey your parents
Santa won't come Christmas Day

Do everything that you are supposed to
The voices they do say
Be a good child for your parents
Santa's coming Christmas Day

Hospital Christmas

The wards were now half empty
Only the truly sick remained
You could tell that it was Christmas
By the lights and candy cane

The Emergency Room was busy
With Diabetes and Depression
Bleeding Ulcers were in season
With this highly stressed recession

Everyone seemed really happy
To end another year
Christmas is for the giving
Happiness and good cheer

The staff at this fine hospital
Providing sustenance and support
Caring for each patient
Christmas cheer and shift report

For those who work on Christmas
Special people who do a lot
Giving and sharing for others
That's what they do, and some do not

Merry Christmas to this hospital
And all the staff therein
To work Christmas in the hospital
Is above and beyond, Amen

Christmas Celebration

Christmas Oh Christmas
Time to light the tree
It's been another year
At Fallen Timbers you see

Smiles and good manners
Feelings of good cheer
They're not just at Christmas
It's all through the year

We practice our profession
With a staff we like a lot
Caring and sharing for patients
Whether they have or have not

But Christmas is Christmas
It's time to reflect
We've done a good job
And have our patient's respect

For each and every member
Of this medical staff you see
Wonderful and caring people
Who care as much as we

Mother Poem

Mother of the poem
Publisher of the thought
Provider of the forum
That we have often sought

Parent to our expression
Poetry, song or prose
Stranger, friend or relation
This forum is what she chose

We read our soliloquy
With feelings and humility
Some shout with great antipathy
But she always shows her empathy

Appreciation for the thought
Delivered at this forum
The platform often sought
Thank you Mother Poem

Annie

Her creations bloomed like the flowers
Her thoughts were applied to the pen
In eternity she creates per infinity
Loving thoughts that forever bloom again

My Poetry

To make one really laugh
To make one want to think
To consider an options carefully
To develop inner strength

To appreciate what's right
To consider what is wrong
To work through depression
To become very strong

The crisis of today
The source of our sorrow
The acceptance of today
The growth of our tomorrow

The Dictionary

I went to the dictionary
To look up a mighty word
Flipped through the many pages
Found a noun and a special verb

To write one's thoughts on the paper
To express them in a special way
To grasp the attention of the reader
To visualize what you have to say

Mr. Webster wrote the dictionary
He entered all the words that he could
Words are the tool of the writer
To use them they must be understood

Down Through the Ages

Down through the ages, the eons of time
Tales have been told by a word and a rhyme
Reflections of the present, mirror of the past
The Muse will portray it and that's his essential task

Mirror of the mind, feeling of the soul
Questions all the answers, Illumination is his goal
The taste of sweet and sadness, to touch what's hot or cold
To question all the madness, make sense of tales of old

Symbols of the moment, a man or woman you see
Not what they are, but what they seem to be
Structure of the family, culture of the past
A strong and positive culture can make the family last

Chameleon

Chameleon of the art, His senses
Are in apparent, but sharpened at the
Heart. The Muse is
present in the most inappropriate way
His rhyme reaches

into your soul
Your Karma of the continuum
of your time. The details of your
existence is fodder for
the thought. Is it
surrealistic or
imagery that is
surreptitiously
sought. A window to your
existence, many segments
of the whole, many
segments do make a picture that
this Muse elicits for the soul

I Almost... Maybe... Saw a Flying Saucer

It was almost forty years ago -- 1954. I was recently
discharged from the US Navy where I had spent four years.
I had been an enlisted man specializing in electronics.

The Korean War was over. As a veteran, I had my G. I. Bill
and planned on a college education. I thought that I needed
to earn some more money before going to school full time.
With this in mind, I enrolled in school part time in South
Bend, Indiana. Employment was obtained with Bendix
Aviation Corporation as an Electronics Technician. Good
technicians were hard to find and they welcomed my skills in
the engineering department. I wanted to be a Physicist. This
job would be good experience for me before transferring to
the Indiana University campus in Bloomington.

Bendix Aviation at that time was developing an electronic
fuel injection carburetion system for jet aircraft. Most of their
contracts were military or government supported. Working in
such a facility required a background check by the FBI. I
had been cleared for "Top Secret" in the service so this was
not a problem.

One day, during my tenure at Bendix, a Canadian company I
remember as the AV. Roe Corporation sent representatives to
Bendix. Their company was developing experimental aircraft
in Canada. They wanted to try out the electronic fuel injec-
tion carburetion system that Bendix had developed.

My bosses in the engineering department called me in and
advised me that I was to accompany the equipment to
Canada. I was introduced to the men from Canada and the
trip began. Even though I was a veteran and had seen a lot of
the world, I was still only 23 years old. The trip seemed
exciting and I looked forward to it.

We drove a large truck up into Canada. At the end of the day we stopped in a city which may have been Toronto. From there we seemed to drive straight north for a very long time. The roads became dirt and eventually were snow covered. Most of the cars we saw had chains to travel the road.

During what seemed to be the middle of the night, we arrived in this small community. They told me it was called Wolf Lake. The truck was unloaded in this large warehouse. I later assisted some technical people in setting up the equipment.

Some of the Canadians seemed to be upset at my presence. They felt that an American had no reason to be there. After much arguing and some phone calls, they accepted me with some reluctance. They wouldn't allow me to inspect the rest of the warehouse or some of the other buildings. There was one very large building which seemed large enough to be a hanger. I never got near it.

The technical people asked me some questions about the equipment. They seemed to know what they were doing. I thought they were just being polite.

Later we were taken to this private home. There were no hotels. The next day we drove back to civilization. I caught a plane in Toronto and returned to South Bend.

Two years later I was actively completing my degree in Physics at Indiana. My professors had given me a job maintaining the electronics and computers in the Physics Department. I might mention that transistors were not invented yet and this was the day of vacuum tubes. A major part of my time was spent in the Physics building and the Physics Library.

While looking through some journals, I noticed an article about the AV. Roe Corporation in Canada. The article stated that the AV. Roe Corporation at an unnamed site in northern Canada had developed an experimental "Flying Saucer." There was a picture in the magazine. It further stated the project was being abandoned as a failure. It stated that the saucer was very fast and highly maneuverable, but they had not been able to control it in flight. The craft was considered unsafe for further research or development

I wondered then as I do now. Did I almost -- maybe -- see a flying saucer? Did they really abandon the project? Sometimes I scan the sky at night and wonder whatever happened to that electronic fuel injection carburetion system from Bendix.

Up in the Arctic

We were up in the Arctic
Trapped in the ice
Two ships of the line
Very cold was the price

Our hull was reinforced
To handle the load
It could break through the ice
Without damage we were told

We'd delivered our cargo
To and outpost with care
Now ready to go home
But the ice kept us there

Over the Arctic circle
You become a "Blue Nose"
An elite membership
For those who would go

Our cargo had been critical
For those stationed there
There wasn't much to do
Except work and do repair

Tending their equipment
Was all they could do
It was a year in the arctic
To replace a new crew

We left them their cargo
It would help pass the time
Ten thousand cases of beer
For these men in their prime

The Armored Vests

Combat vests are protective
But they certainly are heavy
In the heat of the summer
I get uncomfortable and sweaty

No one got hurt
For what seemed a long time
The helmets and the vests
Came off on the line

Someone got hit
And hurt very bad
We grabbed up the helmets
And the vests that we had

Combat vests are protective
And they certainly are heavy
In the heat of the summer
I don't mind being sweaty

Mother Nature

Mother Nature is great. Mother Nature is strong
Sometimes she seems good. Sometimes she seems wrong
She affects all our lives right down to our soul
Coping with her behavior is an astronomical goal
Earth, Wind, and Water affect every life form
Mother Nature controls them. That's simply the norm

Modern Technology is what man has created
Hi Tech and our lives, we seem to be mated
Just when we think we've gained some control
Mother Nature overwhelms us and humbles us low
"Don't mess with Mother Nature", they always did say
She can help you or hurt you on any given day

It's better to work with Mother Nature. Go with the flow
Use what she has to offer but oppose her no more
She provides us with all that we ever could need
Be one with Mother Nature, and don't try to lead

Sunshine

Sometimes I'm up. Sometimes I'm down
Sometimes I smile. Sometimes I frown
The sun comes up, and the sun goes down
I'm always happy when there's sunshine around

The best time for me is the summer of the year
There's lots of sunshine and lots of good cheer
The sun seems to smile on those much longer days
I 'm happy, more positive, when I get my rays

The Fall of the year is still cheerful with sun
Indian Summer, Fall colors, yet full of fun
It's not so depressing when holidays are near
I'll keep up my mood with holiday cheer

Now comes the Winter and the holidays are over
There's very little sun, and the clouds are the cover
Bleak are the days, and cold are the nights
A simple day of sunshine would make my mood
more bright

The next season is Spring and the sunshine is near
Get rid of depression, get new sunshine cheer
Out of our houses, look to the south
Little bits of sunshine is what we're happy about

Our moods are affected by sunshine or its lack
Without the sun, I'd be flat on my back
The happiest time of the year, if you could choose just one
Is the summer of the year with the day's longest sun

The Leaf

The ice has now melted. The frost has left the ground
New life is budding. There are signs all around
The Spring of the year and new life has begun
A bright new life form lays tiny under the sun

His life is exciting. He savors each moment and knows
Like most things in life, with nourishment he will grow
He felt secure at night but looked forward to each day
As he grew longer and wider becoming aware of nature's way

The sun felt good when it shined on his back
He would twist and face the sun wherever it was at
Water felt good and the rain quenched his thirst
He collected more moisture which he drew from the earth

The summer then passed. He no longer felt big and strong
With the coming of the frost, something seemed to be wrong
He shuddered and shivered. This wasn't any fun
The nights became colder. During the day he sought the sun

His color started to change with each freezing night
His coat became dull but some parts became bright
His appendage is brittle. It's no longer supple and strong
His coat is now aged. Something seems to be wrong

He looked all around. His friend is changing too
If only they were together, he wouldn't be so blue
They both suddenly broke loose and settled to the ground
Two leaves and Mother Nature intrinsically bound

Golf

If you are going to play golf
I'll give you advice
Don't hit a hook
Don't hit a slice

It's straight down the fairway
The best place to be
And for goodness sake
Don't hit a tree

I learned to play golf
I took the advice
Didn't hit a hook
But I did hit a slice

It was straight down the fairway
I always tried to be
But more often than not
I'd hit a darn tree

I drove and I putted
Chipped the best I could
But no matter how I tried
It wasn't very good

There was the sand, the deep grass
And this pond you see
And when I came over the hill
There was always that darn tree

Sometimes I wonder
Why I still hit that ball
When you hit a tree
It's no fun at all

But I still play golf
And I still hit that tree
It's the sun and fresh air
And the friends at the tee

A Fish Story That's True

I'll tell you a fish story, a story that's true
When you go out fishing, a story is due
I've fished on the lake, fished on the sea
Fished at a brook where this story will be

I'd caught many a fish, filled my table and more
But the biggest fish I had, was bought in the store
I went to this brook, someone told me the way
Tried every bait and hook but no fish that day

I was about to go home, when up in the air
Jumped the biggest fish ever, none could compare
I worked the surface, with all I could try
But he jumped up again and spit in my eye

He leaped and he circled and teased me some more
I used all my lures and went back to the store
He kept stealing my bait, and I wanted to cry
Then he'd jump up again and spit in my eye

I thought I had hooked him when he jerked on my line
I pulled him in close, and he really looked fine
Then he coughed up the hook, and I let out a cry
He almost smiled when he spit in my eye

I was frustrated then, and thought I would die
I'd tried every hook and lure I could try
Many times in the future, I returned to that brook
He's still there, and he jumps and coughs out my hook

I swear that some day, when I catch this big fish
I'll look right at him and grant his last wish
I'll throw him right back when he lets out a cry
Where else is a fish that can spit in your eye

The Gulf

There were planes up in the sky
There were troops upon the ground
There were tanks and then artillery
There were copters all around

There were troops from our great nation
There were troops from Saudi too
There were both men and women
There was a big job to do

They vowed to free these neighbors
They pledged to do it right
They vowed no more aggression
They formed a new world that night

All nations should stand together
All nations should be free
All nations should respect each other
It's a world of nations you see

We may argue in each country
We may fight and disagree a lot
But each individual nation
Should exist and not be forgot

Doctor My Doctor

Doctor Oh Doctor
Please help my son
He's sick with the flu
His bowels on the run

Doctor My Doctor
My wife's down in bed
The mother of my children
A chronic illness it is said

Doctor Oh Doctor
My daughters with child
We've done our best to raise her
But she's just been too wild

Doctor My Doctor
My husband's depressed
He just lost his job
Now there's pain in his chest

Doctor Oh Doctor
Please help us all
Without you to assist us
There's no one to call

The Fingernail

She came to the office in obvious distress
To the nurse she gave only her name and address
A problem for the Doctor, only he would understand
Most embarrassing to tell, even this medicine man

She had tried and tried to treat it herself
Now she had come to the doctor seeking his help
Something in her nose, it really does bleed
Could he please get it out, in her time of urgent need

He removed the foreign object as quick as a wink
She felt much better but embarrassed to think
That anyone would know what had happened to her
The Doctor had seen it often, but as for him, it never did
occur.

Malpractice

There once was a child who had a bad heart
Born with a defect, a problem from the start
They took him to surgery, a defect to correct
All seemed to go well, it was really Hi Tech

Sometime in recovery, it seemed to go wrong
There was cardiac arrest, the damage was long
The hopes for the future were now very bleak
Consequences of the event, long term rehab to seek

One future was gone, a new one instead
For one angry family, to an attorney it led
These kinds of cases, he just didn't do
But upon observing the child, something was due

He researched the case, every little clue
Applied all his logic, as a lawyer should do
Accumulating the details, expert opinions galore
This fine ethical barrister found the trap door

Using his knowledge, his experience, and his skill
They went to the courts, ready for the kill
He won this tough case like a tried and true knight
The future for this child seems a little more bright

Holding Life's Hand

I was called to the hospital one cold dreary night
To the room down the hall with the family in sight
The patient was dying, "No Visitors Allowed"
A white haired old man had created this row

He understood the orders, but his face was very grave
He explained their lifetime together, now she couldn't
be saved
He simply needed to be with her, just to please hold
her hand
I simply couldn't refuse him, this strong white haired
gentle man

She died soon thereafter, calm and at ease
The presence of her husband made that easier you see
Gathered in the hall among the family waiting for him
Was a strong tall young man, the very image of him

He stood very tall, strong and with pride
Protectively holding the hand of the bride by his side
The love of a spouse, the strength of a man
Is really quite evident when holding life's hand

His Life Was His Family

He marveled at life, when the children were born
A miracle of God he thought perfect in their form
They grew and developed, fine adults they became
With his God for his guidance, he raised them the same
They appreciated all life as God's special blessing
Experienced it all, life and its testing

His life was his family, his work and his God
Then they found his cancer, time had given its nod
He didn't even hesitate, when told there's no cure
He could marvel at death, if his family was near
The end of his life is a miracle too
We helped him stay home, to experience what's due

All life is a blessing from birth to the end
The good lord allows the Doctors to attend
And when someone special appreciates all life
We'll treat them, support them all through their strife

Alice May

You're a very special person
A very special friend
You're there when you are needed
A helping hand to lend

There's a few years left to go
We'll work together till then
But even after retirement
You'll always be my friend

The Need for a Smoke

As was my custom, I arose at pre dawn
Loose clothing, sneakers and
stepped out into the morning
I was at a hotel
In a Midwestern University City
As I started my morning walk
My senses filled with the morning
High on life
Joggers on the walk
Other walkers
Smokers huddled in the doorways
On the bench
No restaurants open at this early hour
This time of day I gathered my thoughts
Stretched out my body with the signs of arthritis
Greeting the day as a blessing, an opportunity
To create something new
To continue or change something old
I thanked that unknown power
For granting me another day

After completing my morning
I walked back towards the hotel
The shops were all open
The walks and streets teeming with activity
The business of the day in full pursuit

In the late afternoon, the panorama changed again
The active people of the day were
less active
Walking more slowly or
Hurrying somewhere different

The students were now all around the square
Active, shouting, challenging life
A band played on the sidewalk
A small group looked on
A speaker on a small platform
Shouting obscenities
A crowd gathered around
Shouting their support
The world needs changing
It will be their world .....
someday
The restaurants were busy
People relaxed
Sharing their evening repast
An interlude
Away from home
Small clusters of unshaven
Smoking, antisocial imaged
Individuals discussed their day in court
Their odds of dealing with
or beating the system

Their attorney's only tolerated
A necessity
They seemed defiant
Defensive
Angry
Powerful

Later, I walked back to the hotel
The street people
Settling into the doorways
The atmosphere more subdued
The smokers
individually or in pairs
Standing outside the hotel
Filling their lungs to the brim
Is it enough to last the night?

Sometimes, I still feel the need for a smoke
Just maybe

The Newborn

I went to the nursery, a baby to check
They bathed him and draped him,
examination set
I poked him and probed him
every possible part
Checked his eyes, ears and lungs, and even
his heart

A healthy new baby, was my final
impression
I breathed with relief, a normal examination
Explained to the parents, that the baby was good
Mother nature should make them all that way,
if only she would

They come in all sizes, shapes and conditions
All Apgar 9,9's, would be a happy rendition

Pitocin

The droplets are falling, the pain is severe
The droplets are falling, the next pain is near
The droplets are falling, try to relax
The droplets are falling, pain at the max
The droplets are falling, panting very fast
The droplets are falling, how long will it last

The pain now is constant, the pressure severe
The pain now is constant, the big one is near
The pain now is constant, the last one is here
The pain now is constant, the reason is clear

She cried with a smile, the old pain is gone
She cried with a smile, a new life begun
She cried with a smile, it came with the dawn
She cried with a smile, and named the baby "Sean"

It's 6 lb. 7 oz, it came in the night
It's 6 lb. 7 oz, it's the parent's delight
It's 6 lb. 7 oz, a new life begun
It's 6 lb. 7 oz, new crying, a new son

The Gallbladder

Pain in the belly, soon nausea to vent
Indigestion the precursor, belching came and went
Fatty food intolerance, bloating now and then
Pain between the shoulder blades, I needed to mend

Went to the doctor, asked about my stool
Admitted light and floating, symptoms to rue
Diagnosis, gallbladder, cholelithiasis by name
Echo gram showed the gallbladder stones all the same

Referred to a surgeon, a new technique he will do
Microscopic surgery, laparoscope the tool
In and out of the hospital, it really was quick
Better than the old way, big incision, very sick

Fever and Cough

Fever and cough, the muscles do ache
Sweats and deep chills, a pill soon to take
Sick for several days, it's not going away
Time to see the Doctor, before another day
She came to the office, seeking help at last
Needs to get better, put symptoms in the past

A temperature is present, the throat it is red
She took all the remedies, home and in bed
I looked in her ears, her throat and her nose
Listened to her chest, no rales for a foe
Abdomen soft, good bowel sounds today
Time to check for strep, keep it away

Her strep test is negative, I let out a smile
Good advise modern medicine, will help for a while
She'll be better tomorrow, if everything's right
Good treatment, good medicine, everything is bright
She'll go back to work, do good for a while
Till the next time she's sick and loses her smile

The Wee and the Bee

She came to the church
Apologetic and in duress
I needed to look at her husband
Who was in some distress

We left the Sunday church meeting
And went to her home
He didn't give much greeting
His pain set the tone

He had felt good after supper
Eating and drinking his fill
But soon he had a full bladder
So he walked down the hill

He strolled to that little small cubby
It was down by the still
Entered that half moon building
To relieve his bladder of its fill

He had unzipped his pants for relief
Anyone could plainly see
But among the other inhabitants
Was this little giant honey bee

He was stung by the bee
It swelled big as a ball
He doubled up with pain
Full bladder and all

I gave him two shots
And took down the swelling
No man should suffer this
But it's a tale worth the telling

Government and Insurance

Insurance and the government
Really don't want to pay
So it's more and more paper work
Like hurdles to jump and complete
each day

They say that they're here to help you
To provide you with universal care
But when it comes to paying the bills
Your money they keep and don't share

You need a test or procedure
It's promised and that seems quite right
But they neglected to tell you it's rationed
Your name's down the list out of sight

We'll give you the best care that's possible
Though they've tied one arm and a hand
The relationship between a Doctor and his Patient
Though damaged it will always stand

Wait Before Light

I opened my eyes in the dark of the night
Went out on the grass to wait for the sight
Gray before orange and then it was light
The miracle of each day was welcome and
bright
I drank of my coffee with a little bit of
white
Ready to start a new day it all seems so
right

My thoughts needed sorting to start a new
day
There were tasks to be done, many things
I had to say
After my shower I'll be on my way
Examining and treating problems
wherever they lay
I got in my car and drove down by the bay
Went to the hospital to make everyone ok

The day was completed, time to go home
A full day of illness has really set the tone
Completing my paperwork, I now stood
alone
Contemplating illnesses and fractures
of the bone
I close up the charts still standing alone
Another day was finished and time to go
home

Back at my house, the light before dark
Sitting on the patio seeing orange before dark
The evening was here, an obvious remark

The day had been good, helping others
that's right
Now we'll finish this day and start a new
night
Tomorrow's a new day, we hope to see the light

Five to Nine

Most of the time, we work nine to five
But with all the new taxes, it's now five to nine
Up in the morning, before the crack of dawn
Home after sundown, cannot even mow the lawn

Work for the tax man till just after noon
No time for lunch, paper work's due soon
Work then till three to pay utilities and rent
It's been a long day and the energy's spent

From three to five it's pay for the staff
Five to six health insurance, that's a laugh
Then six to eight, finally something for me
Wait a minute, eight to nine is a new tax you see

Home after nine, paperwork still due
Need to complete it, so people won't sue
Weekend with the family, a thing of the past
With paperwork and taxes, families don't last

The Doctor is a Lady

The Doctor walked briskly down the long hospital hall
Entered the nurse's station as the physician on call
Reading the notes and the tests that were on the chart
It was quite clear that this patient had a very bad heart

The prognosis was guarded, the treatment quite clear
The patient was ill and the end could be near
The Nurse and the Doctor walked quietly to the room
It was hoped that the suffering would certainly end soon

The Doctor took his hand, the patient started to smile
He knew the Doctor cared, and that made it worth while
No matter what the problem, no matter what the malady
It's nice to get attention, when the Doctor is a Lady

She's professional, considerate, practices state of the art
To have her for your doctor, you get a head start
Admired and respected, she's second to none
Next to all she stands tall, when any day is done

The Stroke

A pang of sensation, burst inside of my head
A partial loss of vision, a stroke it is said
It comes in all forms, some large and some small
A bit of bad fortune, for one and for all

A temporary spasm, minute symptoms, then gone
TIA is a warning, of bad things still to come
The treatment is simple, the rewards undenied
A simple little aspirin, it's all that's applied

A clot from the heart, a plaque from the vessel
Shoots up to the brain, and all is not well
An embolus is formed, cerebral the type
An infarction created, to compromise the life

Thrombosis of the vessel back pressure to the brain
Diagnose it early, the patient is having pain
Some strokes are treatable, don't waste any time
Let's treat them early, don't draw the line

The worst thing to have, give hemorrhage its due
Blow out of the vessel leaking into the tissue
Permanent damage may develop, a life compromised
Sometimes they recover, lay damaged or die

No life is perfect, but some things can be done
Identify your risk factors, multiple or one
Treat what you can, knowing what you can do
Get on with your life, but treat your risks too

The Guardian Angels

They're the Guardian Angels
The light of our lives
These professional nurses
Caring and in white

They support and they help
Giving to those in need
When it comes to patients
They are always in the lead

We love them a lot
These nurses who care
They're the Guardian Angels
We know that they're there

A Life of Service

To live a life of service
To help one's fellow man
Be good to one another
Be the very best you can

A life of helping people
Serving their needs, that's good
Giving of yourself to others
Deeds and spirit you really should

Train yourself how to be noble
Provide your life with a goal
The care and nurturing of others
Is food and wine for the soul

A Lifetime of Effort

My fears have been many, my trials very long
Having dealt with the many, now mostly gone
Many imperfections, put myself to the test
Now satisfied, that I can deal with the rest

A lifetime of effort, a very long school
Dealing with imperfections, learning the golden rule
Liking yourself as a person, first step to success
Reaching out to others, just doing your best

To do your job well, a very good thing
Satisfaction and effort, can make one's heart sing
But even more important, before life is gone
Sharing with someone special life's "old sweet song"

The Phobia

Afraid of crowded places
Afraid of simple heights
Afraid to drive a car
Afraid of just what might

A fear of small closed spaces
A fear of what might be
A fear of objects and places
A crippling disease you see

Agoraphobia, Claustrophobia
And the other phobias too
To have a fear of something
What is a person to do

You can go to psychotherapy
You can take a medicine too
But sooner or later to face it
That's what phobias have to do

Divorce

I've been a physician
A long time it's true
And to deal with an attorney
I'd rather have the flu

But a few years ago
Downtown Toledo I came
I needed an attorney
My life was in pain

I was lost and confused
My life down the drain

I searched and I sought
For an attorney to care
As luck would have it
I found two, that's a pair

They gave me their all
They gave me their best
Winner or loser
It put life to the test

They did what they could
I appreciated it all
I'm a better man today
Than when I came down that hall

These two have now married
I think that's real nice
I hope their life is exciting
Not just sugar and spice

So here's to the bride
And here's to the groom
The two nicest people
In any court room

May their life be long
And enjoy their two sons
May the world have more justice
When two work as one

The Forgotten Father

The forgotten father, is a man
Demeaned and denied by most
He works and he struggles
Best that he can
To care and provide, that's his post

He struggled and he gave in the
marriage
Working to do what was right
He certainly was a good father
But she took away his rights in a fight

She wouldn't let him see his children
There was always some flimsy excuse
She raised them afraid and away from him
Treating him with obnoxious abuse

He went to the court for assistance
Sympathetic and understanding they were
They couldn't really help with his problem
It was something that wouldn't occur

He had placed his trust in the system
That's all that most men can do
But when they made the final decision
It was simply more child support due

She thinks she's the perfect mother
Keeping that horrible man away
The children's minds are now damaged
Though they realize the truth this day

Any bonding has gone by the wayside
The years have prevented that too
All anyone ever remembers
Is more and more child support due

The Father had been responsible
He was empathetic and caring too
All he wanted to be was a father
Bonded with his children and true

Now that's out, and now he's a pauper
There's really nothing more he can do
Sometimes it really doesn't pay to be proper
And there's still more child support due

She's Pretty and She's Spunky

She's pretty and she's spunky
Alive and built with charm
I dream of her often
To hold and to feel in my arms

She's feisty, a rebel, stubborn to the core
Love her, adore her, come back for more
Faithful and Exciting, she's one of a kind
Work hard to keep her, a very good sign

Difficult to keep her
Keep trying all I can
Wouldn't want to hurt her
Just give her my hand

The Sixteenth of January

It was the sixteenth of January
I married this Lady
It was a definite yes
Not a no or a maybe

I'd do it again
Despite trials and trepidation
The good and the bad
She's my life, my sensation

A companion to me
A friend who is true
For the rest of our lives
I'll give her what's due

Happy Anniversary
To the love of my life
I'm glad that you agreed
To be my true wife

The Wedding Toast

Here's to the bride
Here's to the groom
The happiest couple
In the entire room

May their life be happy
May their marriage be long
May their home be filled with children
May their house be filled with song

As the years do come
And the years do go
May their everlasting life together
Be food and drink for the soul

And as they grow older
May they say once again
If I had it to do over
I'd marry you again

Yourself You are Filled

Yourself you are filled with distrust and full
scorn
A barrier to all, your mind made of thorns
No one can get near you, alive or even dead
Most of the time there's just one in our bed

You've protected yourself from all and from
me
This shell of protection from hurt we can see
Angry and critical, a very good defense
To try to get near you just doesn't make
sense

Make no excuses, your mind it is set
The walls of protection won't shield you just
yet
A barrier from hurt, if it should suddenly
appear
Cannot be stopped if you just look in the
mirror

My Needs Are Not Great

My needs are not great, but certainly not
small
I work my profession, satisfaction to all
A very good person, I do what is right
But sharing my life, I need someone at
night

I've seen many people but only need one
To light up my life, like rays from the sun
My work it is hard, but then when it's done
I'll share what I have, for a smile from the
sun

It's possible to live, alone and content
It's even better to share a room and the rent
Needing somebody, as natural as can be
Living alone is ok, but simply not for me

Chains on the Mind

Chains on the mind, torture of the soul
Keeps many an individual from achieving
their goal
Learn what you can, seek the very best
advice
Wisdom comes slowly, not a roll of the
dice

Study your art, your trade and your work
There's never a task, from which you
should shirk
Apply what you learn, be all you can be
Undo those chains, a success you will see

Be good at what you do, respected by all
Accept what you do, as important to all
Wisdom from experience, frees up the
soul
Every little cog, helps us function as a
whole

My Sister Rose

She married my brother a long time ago
They were meant for each other
We all knew it was so
His name was Louis, Her name is Rose

I was just a small child in this family of ours
I learned to adore her this new sister for hours
His name was Louis, Her name is Rose

Their children did grow, and I did grow too
Her family, some married and theirs are now due
My brothers name was Louis, her name is Rose

This lady is special, she gives and loves a lot
She has children, grandchildren
and great grandchildren due
His name was Louis, her name is Rose

She has always been strong, giving care when it's due
She has shouldered life's burdens
And carried them through
My brother's name was Louis, her name is Rose

She's a very special lady, a flower above all thorns
The thorns are almost gone now
She blooms like a tulip's horn
Happy birthday dear sister
Your name could only be Rose

Triplets

They were born and numbered three
They were thought of as one
These three beautiful girls
Born under an August sun

The year's "91" and now they're sixteen
They try to be free but still act as one
These three wonderful girls
Born under an August sun

It's time to be young women
Each different yet they're three
These three beautiful girls
Born under an August sun

They will each go their own way
Becoming separate when they're done
These sixteen and three
Born under an August sun

No matter where they go
No matter what they do
These three will be together
And yet live apart too

I'll love them forever
These daughters three and one
These three wonderful girls
Born under an August sun

The Flashing Red Light

He pulled up beside me with his flashing red light
Jumped out of the car to read me my rights
Standing then behind me, my number to take
He wrote it down quickly and then ran the make

Stepped up beside me, "get out of the car"
Gave me directions, "walk the line on the tar"
I walked down the line, I thought straight as can be
But he still wrote the ticket, a warning for me

"Sir, you really shouldn't drive in the condition you are in
To drive under the influence should be a sin
I'll give you a warning just this one time
Lock your car and be seated in this patrol car of mine"

He drove me home quickly, pulled into the drive
I'd made it home safely and still was alive
"To Protect And To Serve" said the sign on the door
It seemed the young officer had done that and more

He helped me upstairs and into my bed
I wished he'd just left me in my car instead
My wife told the officer as he went out the door
See you soon son, you're a good officer and more

The Year Twenty Nine

The time was depression, the year twenty-nine
On July the 11th was born this brother of mine
Born at Mercy Hospital, Des Moines was the city
Delivered by Daniel Crowley, Mom sure did look pretty

Two years later a little brother was born
Grew up to idolize his brother each morn
A big brother he was, he still remains true
Very special to me, I'll give him his due

He's good with his hands, exceptional in mind
He's accomplished a lot, he's strong and he's kind
Now he's retired, a hobby his life
Turning out wood sculptures, very good with a knife

We live far apart, July the 11th is near
I'll wish him happy birthday, a year of good cheer
If I should ever need him, he'd be by my side
This very special brother, I claim with much pride

The Man From Toledo
(Lyrics from the song)

The man from Toledo, He fought in the war
He served with the forces to even the score
The girl from Toledo served in the war too
She stood right beside him and gave them their due

The man from Toledo worked this job and that
He worked here and there but he never hung his hat
The girl from Toledo she worked here and there
Just working beside him was all she could care

(chorus)

The man from Toledo he loved this young girl
He dove in the ocean and found her a pearl
The girl from Toledo she loved this young man
Accepted the pearl and it went on her hand

The man from Toledo is now home for good
Tried to settle down and he now knew he could
The girl from Toledo she settled down too
A life next to him was the life that she knew

(chorus)

The man from Toledo we'd all like to be
Happy near the shore of that lake named Erie
The girl from Toledo we'd all like to see
The one who stood by him on land and the sea

The man from Toledo he married this girl
He thanked the fine day that he gave her that pearl
The girl from Toledo she married this man
She still has the pearl and it rests on her hand

95

Chorus:

The world is your oyster, the fields are in clover
The diamonds just lay there for someone to take
He dug all the ditches, he got all the riches
And now he's come home to Toledo to stay

The man from Toledo was five feet and ten
He roamed the world over and came home again
The girl from Toledo was five feet and five
She roamed the world over to be by his side

The Girl in My Dream

The girl in my dream
She's pretty, she's smart
She fills up my life
When asleep in the dark

I've loved her forever
She fills up my night
While I lie there sleeping
She makes everything right

I've walked on the moon
I've been to the stars
Dove in strange oceans
Mined diamonds on Mars

But I'd trade all I've done
Give up all I've seen
To spend the rest of my life
With the girl in my dream

For the girl of my dream
The diamond of my life
Is back home on mother Earth
And I'd make her my wife

The Universe is my playground
A star is my child
The Earth is the planet
Where sunshine is mild

I've walked on the moon
I've been to the stars
Dove in strange oceans
Mined diamonds on Mars

But I'd trade all I've done
Give up all I've seen
To spend the rest of my life
With the girl in my dream

The Best That You Can Be

Some of us are weak
Some of us are strong
Some of us are right
Some of us are wrong

Some of us work hard
Do the very best we can
Some of us do just "good enough"
Expect less from our fellowman

No matter what you do
No matter how you try
Do the very best that you can
That's right, that's strong, that's why

Skied Down the Hill

I skied down the hill as fast as can be
Enjoying the day, the hill and the trees
All of a sudden, I unweighted my skis
Up and then down, sudden pain in the knee

Helped down the hill, very slow and in pain
Taken to a hut, ski patrol was the name
A crack in the cartilage, inside of the knee
No more skiing this day, a good doctor to see

I went home on crutches, some wraps on
my leg
Sought out a physician, his opinion to take
Correction of the meniscus, soon to be done
Next year I shall ski in the wind and the sun

Money

I made a lot of money, spent a lot of dough
Didn't save a dime, now I'm feeling low
Thought I really needed, every time I spent
Now I have no money, cannot even pay the
rent

My parents always told me to make a lot of
dough
But no one ever taught me to use some self
control
I spent a lot of money, had a really good time
Now my money friends are gone, not a very
good sign

So if you are going to work, and make a lot of
dough
Spend some of the money but learn some self
control
It's not how much you make or how you really
spend
It's how much you save that matters in the end

A Father and Friend

Father to his children
Husband to his wife
Successful in business
He toils all his life

A pillar of the community
To church, mason, and more
Gives of himself to others
Charitable to needy and poor

A friend when you're in trouble
A friend when you're in need
Yet time for fun and friends
A full life does he lead

I Feel

I feel like an ancient
I feel like a child
I note that I'm lonely
In the middle of a crowd

I like to be noticed
Really want to be free
If I could be happy
And not lost you see

Maybe tomorrow
I'll feel like a man
Positive and productive
Happy, not mad

Hopefully, tomorrow
I'll get a new job
Unemployment makes me
Feel like a slob

The Pharmaceutical Rep

It started with the Shaman, a very long time ago
They used plants and animal parts, our history tells us so
They passed along their knowledge, generations by the score
Until multiple concoctions created chemists at the local
Pharmacy Store

To create all these chemicals, then to distribute, and sell to all
Evolved the Pharmaceutical Industry, as we quite readily recall
They manufacture their products for distribution and sale
But to get them to the patient is a long and ardurous trail

The Pharmaceutical Representative, a special link in the
chain
Between the chemical manufacturer, the patient and his pain
They call on the drugstore, the hospital, and Doctors by the
score
Getting the product to the patient, takes the Reps and
very much more

A good product is critical for treatment, really important to all
Getting it to the patient, requires representatives who can
certainly make the call
A new and exciting medicine, was the best that he had seen
But to get the Doctor's attention, no small task by any means

It takes skill, knowledge, fortitude, and patience at every
difficult step
To bring that product to the Doctor, so that he won't forget
A service to the Doctor, the patient and the store
The Pharmaceutical Representative, provides service
when he calls at any office door

Sixty Years Old

I woke up in the morning
With a buzz in my head
Hardening of the arteries
Causing tinnitus it is said

Walking across the room
All bent over with an ache
It's the start of arthritis
Come on, give me a break

Frequent micturition
The prostate is getting big
No hair on my head
I like it and don't want a wig

It's time to look back
And see what I've become
A junior senior citizen
Arteriosclerosis on the run

I'm more blessed that most
A good life I've had
No matter what happens
The good and the bad

I've done many things
Some happy, some blue
But being a Physician
I've given my due

I'm gifted with friends
I think their real swell
They've stood by me and for me
Even though it's been hell

But the best thing I've had
Is Helen, my wife
She came with two sons
And decorated my life

So here's to my family
A wife and two sons
And now daughter in law, Keri
I feel life has just begun

Life Can Be True

Life can be tragic. Life can be true
Sharing with another, it's then not so blue
An exciting new friend, an understanding
spouse
Shout to the heavens, be quiet as a mouse

The ideal situation to deal with your life
Support from your husband, love of your
wife
Days can be cruel, nights can be bad
Sometimes it's easy, sometimes it's sad

To pick where you live and like what you do
To share it with someone you really love true
There's no more to life, no need to be
Real happiness is simple for an who would
see

Little Pete

He was brought to the office
In his uniform and in pain
He had fractured his arm
In an afternoon game

His clothes were all dirty
His cleats off his feet
He'd played the game fully
This little man they called "Pete"

His fracture was set quickly
His arm placed in a cast
It was super double thickness
We hoped the cast would last

Only three days later
"Pete" was back in the room
His cast was in fragments
He'd practiced much to soon

We put on a new cast
Triple strength and double sling
But with little guys like this
That doesn't mean a thing

By the end of the month
I'd lost track of all the casts
Because with guys named "Pete"
There's no cast that will last

He's cute as can be
The guys only age nine
With or without a cast
He'll play ball any day or time

The Grain Feeder

Standing in the barn, feeding of the grain
Sometimes it's boring, sometimes a pain
The old grain feeder, very old indeed
It sure does the job, all I could ever need

My thoughts were wandering, one night in the barn
The grain feeder was waiting, to set off my alarm
An old bolt stuck out spinning on the end
It spun and it moved faster than the wind

It then grabbed my shoelace, as it spun all around
Caught and stripped my jeans, as it whipped me to
the ground
I was flat on my back, in half of a blink you see
Old jeans tear easily, or feed I would be

I picked myself up, almost naked you could see
A few abrasions and embarrassed, that's certainly me
Now a new plastic guard on the machine works just fine
Machines need attention too, just like people in kind

Carcinoma

Powerless to change it
The end will come soon
The pain seems unbearable
In the long and late afternoon

Evening seems much more tolerable
With friends or a caring spouse
No need for that extra medicine
When there are others in the house

Carcinoma comes to many
It occurs in a variety of forms
For some it means pain and misery
For others, wasting is the norm

Some cancers seem to grow quickly
Others seem to grow slow
But once you've made the diagnosis
Your life changes, forever more

The "Power of Positive Thinking!"
Norman Vincent Peale wrote a long time ago
It's helped many people, many patients
No matter how the tumor seems to grow

To accept what you have to
To treat what you really can
Live life to the fullest
Be a special grain in the sand

110

Sports Doctor

Swelling of the ankle
Fluid on the knee
Shaking spasm in the muscle
Tendons tight you can see

Ice the swelling quickly
Rest and brace a lot
Tomorrow is another day
To give it all that you've got

The Sport Doctor's hands are sure
They probe and find the cause
They help you recover quickly
Not even time to pause

A shot to kill the pain
Rehab till it's just right
The race will come tomorrow
The gold that shines so bright

Physician to the family
Healer of the best
Diseases of some patients
Injuries put to rest

Medication and ice
Heat and ultrasound
First reduce the swelling
Range of motion all around

Stretch the tissue slowly
Build the strength to pound
Ambulate them quickly
Rehab is hallowed ground

111

1994

The "Eternal Flame" is brought from afar
High up above, it's bright as a star
The athletes come to compete and attend
Many nations, many medals, chance to make a friend

Every four years, the best of the best
Everyone is proud, spectators and the rest
Representing self and nation, all of human kind
Competing for the gold, like a rare and perfect wine

The Skater

Spinning on the ice, laces cut by skate
Little black clouds, more bad luck to take
Show the world you're human, give all you've got
You didn't win a medal, but effort is not forgot

Handle the diversity, learn from a mistake
Be good, yet human, when next time you skate
It's OK to be tough and "throw rocks at the crowd"
But better to be vulnerable and not quite so loud

Learn from the past, get on with your life
Grow with the knowledge to tolerate that strife
Come back in four, the best you can be
Go for the gold, stand tall for all to see

The Racer

Best in the world, medal never won
Try again and again, race into the sun
Flash down the ice, accidents occur
Go home, train again, wait another year

Lots of support, train for the race
New site, new medals, need to set the pace
Last race, last day, last chance, icy cold
What a surprise, new record and the gold

About the Author

Daniel Richard Sullivan, MD. is one of the founders of and practices with Fallen Timbers Family Physicians in Maumee, Ohio. He was born November 18, 1931 in Des Moines, Iowa. In 1937, his family moved to Goshen, Indiana. He grew up there and graduated from Goshen High School in 1949.

After working construction for a year he served four years as an Electronics Technician in the US Navy during the Korean War. Then, he worked two years doing electronics in South Bend, Indiana before going to Indiana University in Bloomington. His degree in Physics was obtained in 1958 and his medical degree in 1962. Hospital training was obtained in Toledo, Ohio. Since that time he has been a Family Physician in the Toledo area. He has an appointment as Clinical Associate Professor of Family Medicine at the Medical College of Ohio. In addition he is an Affiliate of the Cleveland Clinic. He is on active and courtesy staff at several Toledo area hospitals. Dr. Sullivan has six children, including triplets, by his first marriage, and he has two step sons by his second marriage. Being a Grandfather is a truly enjoyable part of his life.

He writes and performs poetry with *The Writers Company* in Toledo. He still practices medicine but would like to do more writing in the future. Seminars have been attended at the "Writers' Festival" at the University of Iowa.

Writing about life, feelings, and experiences of people and their families is his special interest. To provide the reader with a sense of deja vu or identity with his writings would be his most hoped for accomplishment.